Simple
Secrets of
Parenting

Simple Secrets of Parenting

Easy as ABC

By John Q. Baucom
Illustrated by Cathy Abramson

Child & Family Press ❖ *Washington, DC*

Child & Family Press is an imprint of the Child Welfare League of America, Inc.

© 1997 by the Child Welfare League of America, Inc. All rights reserved.
Neither this book nor any part may be reproduced or transmitted in any form or by any
means, electronic or mechanical, including photocopying, microfilming, and recording,
or by any information storage and retrieval system, without permission in writing from
the publisher. For information on this or other CWLA publications, contact the CWLA
Publications Department at the address below.

CHILD WELFARE LEAGUE OF AMERICA, INC.
440 First Street, NW, Third Floor, Washington, DC 20001-2085
e-mail: books@cwla.org

CURRENT PRINTING (last digit)
10 9 8 7 6 5 4 3 2 1

Book design by Wendy Kessler-Effron

Cover design by Sarah Knipschild

Printed in the United States of America

Library of Congress Cataloging-in-Publication Data
Baucom, John Q.
    Simple secrets of parenting : easy as ABC / by John Q. Baucom :
[Cathy B. Abramson, illustrator].
      p.   cm.
    ISBN 0-87868-638-X (pbk.)
    1. Child rearing.   2. Parenting.   I. Title.
HQ769.B38 1997
649´. 1--dc21   97-2301

In memory of my
grandparents Carl and Ethel.
In gratitude to my mother Lois and
my schweigermuter Edwinna.

Introduction

Parenting is important–
vitally important. Obviously, there are many problems
in our world today. Our children face situations on a
daily basis that were unheard of in our generation.

In this book, I've attempted to present some
vitally important principles in a simple, readable
format. I've kept it plain and practical. And I've
included humor, sadness, and a bit of tragedy in this
honest formula because we've all experienced
those things in our own families.

Since 1975, I have worked with married and divorced
parents, blended-family members, single parents,
stepparents, and foster parents. I've met all kinds of
people, I've learned a lot, and I've tried to put what
I've learned into this book.

Accept
Your Child

Acceptance feels good.

Children flourish when acceptance is offered. The most powerful acceptance is unconditional. This means that no matter what your child does, he feels accepted, loved, and nurtured by you. Acceptance communicates to your child that "no matter what you do, I will still love you, and there's nothing you can ever do that will change the way I feel."

Acceptance doesn't mean approving of everything children do. You can accept and love your child without loving his report card. Sometimes it's important to separate the behaver from the behavior. Regardless of his behavior, let your child know he's still loved.

Behave as if You Care

Behavior is active. Attitudes are passive. A behavior is something you can observe or measure. In some way you can see, hear, or experience it. Loving attitudes are nice, but loving behaviors are better. Behaving as if you care means doing something with your child. The more senses you stimulate while doing this thing, the better. The key can be found in the word *intensity*. The more intensely positive the interaction, the more meaningful and real it is to your child. Your child won't believe you care unless you show you care. Just do it and see.

When National Merit Scholarship winners were asked which of their high school teachers was the most helpful, they never named the teacher who was the easiest or hardest or most intelligent. Across the board, the teachers rated most helpful were those who behaved as if they cared. These teachers communicated a one-on-one personal interest in their students' individual welfare. This is the miracle of behaving as if you care.

Catch Your Child Doing Something Right!

Everybody likes attention. I like it. You like it. Children like it as well.

One of your child's basic needs is attention – and she will do almost anything to get it. If she can get your attention for doing something right, she'll do that. If the only way she can get your attention is by doing something wrong, she'll do that too. It's attention that most children are after.

One way to give your child attention is to call her by name when you catch her doing something right. Make a big deal about it. Say, "Claire, get over here! I saw what you did. You helped your brother tie his shoes. That's great. Way to go!"

If you make a big deal only when you catch her doing something wrong, it's not difficult to figure out which behavior will be repeated. If you catch her doing something right, she'll make an effort to get caught doing something right in the future.

Catch her doing something right. Praise her for it. Compliment her. Thank her. Pat her on the back. Get excited. Give her balloons. Bake a cake.

Catch her doing something right.

Don't Push

When you push, it makes people want to push back. Pushing hurts. Pushing creates conflict. Don't do it.

Children today are under enough pressure already. School creates pressure. Friends create pressure. Sometimes, simply surviving creates pressure. So does pushing.

If you push, your child will push back. You'll start an emotional tug of war–one that you'll ultimately lose.

Instead of pushing, send invitations to succeed. Invite your child to try behaviors you know will benefit him in the long run. Invite him to do his homework, join scouts, or join you in volunteer work. If you want your child to try one activity each season–fall, winter, spring, summer–let him choose from a list.

Encouragement is not the same as pushing. Encouragement is enthusiastic, positive, nurturing, and uplifting. Pushing can be threatening and negative. Sometimes, if it's only your goal and not your child's, even encouragement can be pushing. Give your child direction, but let him set his goals.

Enforce Guidelines with Love

Guidelines are important. Children are happiest and healthiest when their parents' responses are reasonably predictable. Structure helps your child make sense of her world. Her life becomes more predictable and therefore less stressful.

Some children with high self-esteem play sports, some don't. Some come from two-parent homes, some don't. Some make good grades, some don't. All children with high self-esteem, however, come from homes where there are guidelines and structure, enforced with love. Their parents have clear expectations and set clear guidelines. They communicate them plainly, and enforce them lovingly.

The most important part of having guidelines is to ensure that they're enforced. Implement your guidelines with love and watch your child's self-esteem grow.

Find Something Your Child Can Excel At

Your child will excel at something.

That's no surprise, right? Everyone enjoys being great at something. Being productive and useful gives purpose and meaning to life. With children, however, excelling is even more significant. Excelling at something is the foundation on which your child builds his self-esteem.

Problems arise when children have no foundation for self-esteem and have found nowhere to excel. Your child will continue looking until he does find something. And it may be using drugs, joining a gang, or stealing a car. Whatever it is, he will excel at something.

At the earliest possible age, help your child find a useful, positive skill at which he can excel. Help him try different things. Have him keep trying until he finds something that interests him. It can be sports, choir, drama, or debate. It can be martial arts, dance, or band. But help your child find something positive at which he can excel. If you don't help him find it, odds are he will excel at something negative.

Give Your Child the Opportunity to Struggle

Why on earth would anyone want their child to struggle?

Children who *aren't* allowed to struggle grow up to believe life should be easy–when facing their first true struggles, they may give up. This often happens when a child breezes by the first three or four grades in school. In the middle grades, when she has to begin to work on her own, she feels like a failure. She decides something must be wrong with her.

Let your child experience firsthand that good things can be hers, but only if she works and waits. One way to do this is to plant a garden together, even if it's only in a flower pot. Start from seeds if possible, and let her weed, water, and take care of her own plants and flowers.

The next time your child wants an expensive item, let her earn and save the money to buy it herself. She may decide that if she has to work for it, she doesn't want it that badly, or she may work, save, and experience the pride of having struggled to earn something she really wants.

Happiness Is Internal

Happiness is inside of us.

To most people, that's a bizarre concept. We've been taught all our lives that happiness is in attaining something. Happiness is in getting the grades, hitting the ball, finding a job, achieving material success.

Wrong!

Teach your child – and yourself – that happiness is something you carry with you. It's a mind-set. It's an attitude. It's not something you see or touch or taste or smell. It's something you believe. And it's something you live.

I often see young children who aren't happy unless they get their way. This usually arises when parents give in to tantrums. Perhaps you're in the grocery store and your child is raising absolute havoc because he wants a toy. If you give in, he becomes quiet, but he's learned two dangerous lessons. The first is how to manipulate you. The second is that happiness is in the toy. Never give in to tantrums. Logic, yes. Tantrums, no.

Happiness is not at the end of a rainbow. It's not in any outside thing. It's something you are.

Invite Your Child to Talk About Problems

In their early years, most children are emotionally honest. Maybe through the influence of Big Bird, they'll tell you when they're mad, sad, or glad. Later, however, they learn to lie or to deny their emotions. That's too bad.

It's important to keep children honest about their emotions. Denying emotional reality can lead to major emotional problems–and to ulcers, headaches, and other medical problems.

Talk calmly about your own emotions. Teach your child to do the same. Discuss this idea with your child. Explain how important it is to be honest about feelings.

Help your child start a "feelings journal." Writing in a journal or a diary is a good exercise for all emotions, especially those that are difficult to express.

Emotional honesty can actually prevent your child from getting into trouble. If she talks about her feelings, she won't become them.

Jump for Joy!
Jog for Self-Esteem!

"Nothing lifts me out of a bad mood better than a hard workout on my treadmill. It never fails;... exercise is nothing short of a miracle."

Cher,
American actress

Let's face it. Kids are tough on each other. They tease and make fun of people who aren't fit. Children who are physically active have higher self-esteem, higher grade-point averages, and better body images than couch potato kids. They like themselves more and are happier.

Especially during adolescence, being part of a team can add tremendous meaning to your child's life, but team sports aren't the only option. Any kind of exercise is great. Get your child moving–walking, swimming, biking, skating. Joining your child in these activities is a great way to bond with him.

The benefits of movement and exercise are infinite.

Keep the Communication Lines Open

Keeping communication lines open means creating an atmosphere where communication is possible. One of the ways to accomplish this is by limiting your criticism. When your child tells you she "messed up big time," and you want to explode, wait until you can react calmly and then respond.

Look at your child when she talks to you. Put the newspaper down. Turn the TV off. Quit eating. Pull the car to the side of the road. If she wants to talk, give her the attention she deserves.

Become a mirror image of your child. Do what she is doing. If she's sitting, you sit. If she's standing, you stand. If her hands are in her pockets, put your hands in your pockets. Listen with your body as well as your ears.

If your child finds it difficult to communicate with you face to face, suggest she write or draw how she feels. Explain that you won't judge what she writes. You want her to be as honest as she can. Sometimes, she'll begin with one idea and end up with something totally different–the real issue. That's okay. The lines of communication will be open.

Listen

Without a doubt, "nobody listens" is the biggest complaint of children in therapy.

Actually, somebody does listen. Drug dealers listen. Oversexed adolescents listen. Child molesters listen. That's why their behaviors are so frequently successful. They know this secret. Now you know it as well.

Normal listening does require your silence. It requires you to periodically nod your head, give an occasional affirming "uh-huh," and be patient. As parents, we often don't have a lot of patience. If you want to help your child, listen without interrupting, without criticizing, and without judging.

A step above normal listening is active listening. Listen closely to what your child is saying. Pay attention to his words and emotions and try to remember what you're hearing. When you respond, clarify or reflect back: "What I heard you say was...," and then repeat or summarize, asking, "Did I hear you correctly?" Again, avoid interpreting, judging, or criticizing what you hear.

This isn't magic, but it's close.

Model What You Want Your Children to Become

Without question, parents exert the most powerful influence on children. Your child learns most effectively by observing and interacting with you. Often, she ends up repeating your behavior, for good or bad.

Model what you want your child to become. You want your child to be happy? Then be happy yourself! Many complex factors contribute to your child's behavior. It's unfair to isolate one and say it's a bigger deal than the others. Over the long haul, however, psychologically healthy parents tend to raise psychologically healthy children.

If you want to help your kids, help yourself. Model what you want them to become. Do you want your daughter to have high self-esteem? Model it. Do you want your son to be able to handle his anger? Model it. Do you want your child to be successful? Model it.

Does this put a lot of emphasis on parents? Yes. Parenting is a tough job. Nobody's perfect. When you make a mistake, you can model another important skill. Apologize. Tell your child you're sorry and then go on with life. It models for her that she doesn't have to be perfect. What a gift!

Negotiate and Compromise

Problem solving, negotiating, and compromising are necessary skills. They're not usually taught in school. If they were, divorce, war, and lawyers would be unnecessary.

To teach your child to negotiate, you need to be able to do it yourself. It comes to some people much more easily than to others. But you do have to work at it.

Negotiation begins with being able to see things from the other person's point of view. If your child is young, begin with questions like, "If you have the biggest piece of cake you'll be happy. But how will your brother feel?" After a while, your child will be able to identify someone else's feelings.

Avoid settling the issue yourself. Using the previous example, you may have to prompt with something like, "How could I cut the cake so you both will be happy?" Or you could say, "You cut the pieces, but your sister gets first choice." That forces a learning about negotiation.

Your child is reaching the age of negotiation about the time you hear him wail, "It's not fair!" Now is the time to teach that fairness applies to others as well as to one's self. The abstract concept of fairness becomes the basis for learning negotiation and compromise.

Offer Opportunities
for Earning

"I do not want anybody to convince my son that someone will guarantee him a living. I want him rather to realize that there is plenty of opportunity in this country for him to achieve success, but whether he wins or loses depends entirely on his own character, perseverance, thrift, intelligence, and capacity for hard work."

John L. Griffith,
American author

Should children get an allowance? I'm asked this question a lot. The answer is a qualified yes. Children should be given the opportunity to *earn* an allowance.

It's one of those answers a lot of parents don't like. Frankly, it's easier to just give your child the money. But that approach creates an expectation that she'll be taken care of simply because she's your child. Big mistake.

We say work is necessary for success. Certainly luck, opportunity, and other factors also come into play. Yet the most significant and the only common element in all success is work. Being your "little girl" is not work. It's happenstance.

If you perpetuate the expectation of being taken care of, you create big problems down the road. One woman told me, "I wish I could go through the 'empty-nest crisis.' I've got a 26-year-old and a 23-year-old at home, plus two grandchildren!"

Give your child every opportunity to earn money. But *earn* is the operative word. Your child deserves an allowance, but she needs to earn every cent of it.

Perception and Positive Thinking

"The difference between a lady and a flower girl is not the way she acts, but the way she is treated. I shall always be a flower girl to Professor Higgins because he always treats me as one and always will. I shall always be a lady to Colonel Pickering because he always treats me as one and always will."

Eliza Doolittle,
a character in *My Fair Lady*

Belief and perception are extremely powerful. The beliefs and expectations of an authority figure – such as a teacher – about a child can alter the outcomes for him. The same is true for parental beliefs.

What are your beliefs about and expectations for your child? If you value and believe in his ability, you will communicate this, even on a nonverbal level. If you believe he can't achieve, in one way or another, that also will be communicated.

Create a positive effect. Communicate positive expectations to your child. Say, "I expect you to put the milk back in the fridge when you finish with it." "I'm pleased that you put back the milk quickly."

Don't use labels when you correct your child. Words such as *clumsy*, *dummy*, or *stupid* are all damaging. Instead, describe your child's behavior. Try, "You acted irresponsibly today when you didn't put the milk away." Be clear about your expectations and describe what's happening now.

Expect great things from your child and he will achieve great things.

Quantity Time Leads to Quality Time

It's a meaningless distinction, yet one I've heard for years. "I don't have much time to spend with my children," parents say, "so I spend quality time with them."

There is no quality time without quantity time! Whoever said you could have one without the other lied. Quality time is great–so long as you don't use it as an excuse for not spending enough time with your child.

Quality time is something you earn through the investment of quantity time. If you deposit quantity time in the bank, you will withdraw quality time later.

Quantity time is driving your child to and from school or activities. It's going to the store together, cooking together, playing catch together, jogging together, watching TV together, or eating as a family. The time spent on these "ordinary" activities provides the closeness and familiarity required for the "quality" moments. Quality moments really aren't planned. They are gifts your child gives to you in return for your quantity time. But you have to be present to experience them.

Quality time is the return on your investment of quantity time.

Recognize Your Child's Personal Best

To travel hopefully is a better thing than to arrive, and the true success is to labour.

Robert Louis Stevenson,
British author

Kids of all ages love being first– the best, the fastest, the biggest, or the smartest.

There's nothing wrong with wanting to succeed. Healthy competition is a great motivator. But competition always produces more losers than winners. Raised in a world of shoulds, musts, and oughts, some children get the idea that they have to be the best to be acceptable. Be sure your child knows that she's "number one" with you even when she doesn't finish first.

Introduce the concept of "personal best." Don't just look at a report card and count the As. Ask: "How do you feel about this grade? Does this represent your best effort?" Sometimes a lot of hard work goes into pulling up to a C. Sometimes a B+ in a nonacademic subject reveals your child's real talent and most honest source of pride. Sometimes an A should have been an A+. It all depends on your child. Every child is uniquely gifted.

Encourage your child to strive. But be sure she also can relax and know that her personal best is good enough. She can–if you can.

Save Yourself...
and Your Marriage

Parenting is not for wimps. It's tough. The stress of parenting has probably been responsible for more ulcers, headaches, and disagreements than any other job on earth.

And now I'm going to say something really unpopular, and probably easily misunderstood. The stress of parenting is possibly responsible for a massive number of divorces. This is not to say children are the problem. They're not. It's parents' inability to deal with the stress of parenting that creates the problem. Parents need regular "R & R"–rest and relaxation.

Sometimes the best thing you can do to take care of your child is to take care of yourself. Yes, parenting is vitally important. At the same time, *you* are vitally important. Put a priority on yourself. Take one night out a week without your child whenever possible. A couple of weekends a year away from your child is good maintenance as well.

Take care of yourself. Then you can do a good job of taking care of your child.

Talk About Feelings

Feelings are incredibly powerful. Wars are fought over them. People are murdered because of them. People overeat, drink too much, and self-destruct—all because of feelings.

On the other hand, feelings are also responsible for some of the greatest creations of humankind. Feelings move people. Our most beautiful works of art, literature, and music would not have been created were it not for feelings. Mozart, Michelangelo, Shakespeare, and scores of others were masters at capturing feelings within their art. But feelings have to be controlled and channeled in a positive direction. Depending on how he deals with them, feelings can hurt your child or improve his life.

Emotions and health—the mind and the body—are connected. Talking about feelings can lower blood pressure, increase healthy blood cell counts, lower heart rates, and increase the efficiency of the immune system.

Talking about feelings works extremely well with children. At about the age of eight, children gain a natural fascination with writing and making lists. Encourage this fascination. Buy a special notebook in which your child can record his feelings and the events of the day. The purpose of these writing exercises is not to preserve feelings for posterity, but to get them out in an acceptable way.

Understand First–
Answer Second

The truth is, parents probably never fully understand children. Parents make the mistake of *assuming* they understand. Then they jump in to try and solve the problem or discipline too quickly.

Answering is easy. Understanding is hard. Unfortunately, most people answer before they understand. The next time your child asks for your attention, take time to really hear what's going on. Wait. Be quiet. Listen with empathy. Experience life through your child's eyes. Strip away all judgment and even your need to respond. Commit to saying nothing until you understand and your child knows you understand.

This approach takes time, patience, and skill. But the response you get by attempting to understand before you answer is worth the investment. Understand first, then answer.

When your child asks a question that requires a complex answer or deals with a sensitive topic, first find out how much she knows. For example, a young girl asked her mother, "Where did I come from?" Her mother embarked on a complicated birds-and-bees lecture. After a few minutes, the daughter interrupted. "But Jeremy said he was from Chicago! Where am I from?"

Don't fill your child's thimbleful of question with an oceanful of answer.

Value
Individuality

Children are like fingerprints. Each one is different, unique, and individual, no matter how alike they seem. To children, their differences are far more important than their similarities. Treat each of your children differently.

Parents often think that what works for one child will work for another. Assembly-line parenting doesn't work. The parts aren't interchangeable.

As a single parent, I have erred occasionally. For example, I have encouraged my different children to play the same sports, simply to make it more convenient for me. Sometimes parents have to improvise. It's still important to value each child's uniqueness and individuality.

It's also important that teachers value your child's individuality. Just because your oldest child was a troublemaker (or a star pupil) does not mean that your next child will be the same. Don't compare your children, don't allow others to compare your children, and discourage your children from comparing themselves.

Sometimes your child will misinterpret a compliment you give to his siblings. He thinks that when you say his sister is a good artist, it means that he is not. Discourage such behavior by explaining that a statement is not a comparison. Assure him you value his talents as well, but he must allow his sister her spotlight.

When (or if) to Spank

To spank or not to spank. It's an old question. The word *discipline* comes from the root word *disciple*. Discipline, used as a verb, means to teach. So the real question becomes, is spanking an effective way to teach your child? The scientific answer is No.

Spanking teaches your child an unhealthy method of dealing with anger. It basically communicates: "When you're upset–hit!" It teaches your child to act out her anger. It also interferes with her development of a conscience. After getting spanked, your child figures she has paid for her misbehavior and feels free to repeat it. Or the spanking may make her angry enough to do something worse.

Another problem is that spanking is a deterrent only when the parent who does the spanking is present. Often, it becomes necessary to escalate the spanking to produce the same effect.

There are better ways. Talking things through and allowing your child to come to her own *ah-hah* is a more effective way of learning. Since many forms of misbehavior are a bid for attention, spending time by herself in a corner away from any stimulation–toys or TV, for instance–is probably consequence enough. Some parents use push-ups, running laps, or walking. Others ask for essays. Afterwards, ask your child to explain why she received those consequences. Make sure she can tell you what she did wrong and what she can do right next time.

eXpedite Your Child's Exit

Independence comes gradually. You give your child independence by slowly, gradually, and methodically allowing him to make his own mistakes, decide what to do with his own time, then venture out and risk being on his own.

Maybe we should take a lesson from the eagle. Eagles, unlike humans, aren't intimidated by the empty nest. From the moment the young bird begins to sprout feathers, it is perpetually nuzzled and eventually nosed out of the nest. Sometimes this occurs about a thousand feet up on the edge of a cliff! As the young eagle begins to drop, it instinctively flaps its wings, attempting to soar away. The mother hovers nearby. At the last moment, if the young one doesn't fly, she will swoop down and catch it in her talons seconds before it hits the ground. What a good model to follow!

You don't want your child to crash and burn. But you do want to nuzzle him out of the nest. Sit down with a piece of paper numbered from 3 to 18. Each number represents a birthday–and added privileges and responsibilities. Age 5 could mean a later bedtime, but it would also include being in charge of emptying the playroom trash can. At 16, if your child adds the privilege of driving the family car, he should also add responsibility for filling the gas tank and keeping the car clean.

Nudge your child and watch him soar.

Young People
Need a Vote

The best way to get people to accept change is to give them a voice in the process. If you want your child to support change in your family, give her a voice as well. Even if she doesn't get her way, she'll feel better about things.

One of the best ways to implement this principle is through family meetings. Even though children may not actively participate in each meeting, the fact they're given a forum is important. Depending on the family, meetings can be held either weekly, biweekly, or on an impromptu basis. Larger families probably should have more frequent meetings.

A special note to blended families: This is one of the most important strategies a blended family can implement. Family meetings should be held weekly during the first year of living together.

Family meetings can be conducted in several ways. They can be "free speech zones," where children are allowed to talk about what's going on; therapy-like sessions, where emotional issues are worked through; business meetings, or any combination of the above. At least once a month, plan the family meeting around a fun activity.

Regardless of form, give your child a voice.

Zero in on Your Own Family!

> *"I have been told it was Margaret Mead who said that with the dawning of the two-TV family, Americans quit communicating. I agree. But I would add that with the arrival of the two-bathroom family, Americans quit cooperating. And with the birth of the two-car family, Americans quit associating. Technology has replaced tradition."*
>
> Dr. John Q. Baucom

Zero in on your own family and build a sense of family tradition. Develop your own family rituals. This can be tricky, and may aggravate your parents or grandparents, but if you take a stand on this issue in a good-natured way, it will pay off in the long run.

Rituals are specific, and have an almost daily nature. The way you get up, eat breakfast, and go to bed all can be ritualistic patterns that have special meaning to your family. Rituals don't have to be serious. They can be funny and bring the zest of shared goofiness to family life. On various occasions, my family has developed rituals for the sake of sharing laughter. When one child developed ringworm, we bought a cake, wrote poetry about the ringworm, and grew closer together. Even silly rituals can build memories that last forever.

Holiday visits to extended family are important, but it's even more important to have some traditions with your own family. Traditions are more seasonal in nature than rituals. Families can have a Thanksgiving tradition, a Fourth-of-July tradition, or a wrestling and football season tradition. Traditions build the same qualities as rituals. They're important. They're vital. And in our society, they are particularly necessary.

A life without rituals and traditions can easily become meaningless. It seems rituals and traditions–especially in times of stress–give a person something to look forward to. They provide hope.

About the Author

 John Q. Baucom, Ph.D., is the father of nine children whose ages range from infancy to young adulthood. He is also a decorated Marine Corps veteran. With graduate degrees in psychology and marriage and family counseling, he has been at various times a paratrooper, a Department of Defense advisor in human relations and leadership, and a college professor. Currently he is director of the Human Resource Center, an international counseling and consulting group headquartered in Chattanooga, Tennessee; a conference speaker and guest expert on parenting; and the host of a local call-in talk show. This is his fourth book for parents.